MERR

THE VILLAGE AND THE DOWNS

Louise Lewis

ACKNOWLEDGEMENTS

Many people have given me encouragement and generous support whilst preparing this book. My special thanks go to Gerry Coates, Eric Elson, Ann and Peter Knee, Frank Phillipson, Mark Sturley and Julie Wileman. Thanks also to Peter Sherwood for the four aerial photographs of Merrow.
In conclusion, my appreciation goes to my parents, Lois and Ray Selby, for giving me a childhood home with a garden gate on to Merrow Downs.

This book was first published July 1998

Copyright © 1998, Louise Lewis

ISBN 0-9533777-0-9

Published by Louise Lewis
"Russets", 38 Heatherley Road, Camberley, Surrey. GU15 3LX.

Printed by
Blackdown Press Ltd.
Fernhurst, Haslemere, Surrey, England.

CONTENTS

LIST OF MAPS, DRAWINGS
AND PHOTOGRAPHS

INTRODUCTION

My reason for producing this little book about Merrow is because I have had a home in Surrey all my life and lived for forty years in a house backing on to Merrow Downs. My aim is to show how the village of Merrow has developed in the last 200 years and to include some facts about the Downs which may not be widely known. At the end I have included some poems about Merrow written since 1840.

LOUISE LEWIS
April 1998

Merrow - 1839. Part of *Guildford Circa 1840* Map produced in 1976 by the
Guildford Group of the Surrey Archaeological Society.

CHAPTER ONE

THE NINETEENTH CENTURY

The map produced in 1976 by the Guildford Group of the Surrey Arch-aeological Society entitled *Guildford circa 1840* provides an overall view of Merrow in **1839**. A copy of this section of the map is at the start of this chapter.

Merrow is one of the villages on the "spring-line" between Guildford and Leatherhead in the centre of the county of Surrey. East and West Clandon, Merrow's neighbouring villages, and other villages on the spring-line owed their origin to the existence of pure water issuing from the surface of the chalk dip-slope at the point where it meets the London clay. This was also an important routeway from earliest times. (Cracknell in *Surrey County Magazine* Sept/Oct 1984, p12)

In the early 19th century the Reverend Owen Manning and William Bray in *The History and Antiquities of the County of Surrey* (Vol.III, p59) gave the following description of Merrow :-

> "It adjoins to West Clandon on the East, to Stoke on the West, to Stoke and Send on the North, and to St. Martha-on-the-Hill and Albury on the South. On the South side it has a large portion of the open Down, over which passes the principal part of the Course on which the Races called Guildford Races are run."

Before the start of the coaching era in the mid-18th century long stretches of Surrey roads were in such poor condition that they were unusable as wagon or carriage-ways. There was a need for better means of communi-cation, especially between London and the south coast. Surrey was becom-ing a sought-after place of residence by people who wished to have conve-nient access to London and, as soon as road surfaces were improved, large houses sprang up near those roads.

A fuller picture of the situation leading up to 1840 is provided by Dr. Peter Brandon in *A History of Surrey*, Chapter XI [Appendix 1] (Brandon, 1977, p71/2/3/5).

In 1758 the road between Guildford and Leatherhead was constructed. About the same time, too, the old roads from Guildford to Farnham along the Hog's Back, and from Guildford to Portsmouth by way of Hindhead were vastly improved. In most cases the turnpike system was introduced: that is to say the improvements were effected by means of a statutory company which was empowered to procure a return for its capital, and a fund for the upkeep of the roads by means of tolls levied at gates situated every few miles along the roads. (Hearnshaw, 1936, p165/6)

The coach road between Guildford and Leatherhead was turnpiked. In Merrow it was known as the Upper and Lower Turnpike Road and these names and the Toll Gate have been marked on the tracing taken from the **1870** Ordnance Survey 6":1 mile map. This map also shows that the hub of the village was **"the crossroads"** [subsequent references to **"the crossroads"** all refer to this junction] at the junction of Merrow Street to the north, Hodds Lane [today's Trodds Lane] to the south and the Turnpike Road. The church of St. John the Evangelist and the Running Horse Inn are on either side of Hodds Lane at this junction. There are several buildings to the north of the Turnpike Road as well as on either side of Merrow Street and a few other buildings on the south side of the Turnpike Road. (The tracing and the **1870** map show these roads.)

Back Lane [today's Park Lane], which is believed to be the oldest road in Merrow, is shown on the tracing and the **1870** map, parallel to and running east of Merrow Street and west of Clandon Park. Merrow Street runs northwards to Merrow Common - open roadside land, with many trees upon it (*Victoria History*, Vol.III, p357). Hodds Lane ran south from the church to the start of the Downs, when it became Albury Way and continued up to Newlands Corner.

In the mid-19th century the parish of Merrow, according to the estimation under the Tithe Commutation Act, comprised only 1600 acres of land; of which 250 acres, forming part of West Clandon Park, were tithe-free by prescription. Of the remainder 783 acres were arable land, 85 acres meadows, 42 acres woodlands and 390 acres commons. (Wedlake Brayley, Vol.II 1850, Walford revision, p301)

The acreage of 4 of the larger farms was as follows:-

Boxgrove Farm (below and opposite Goodwin's Farm) 150 acres.
Great Goodwin Farm (to the east of Merrow Street) 100 acres.
Coxhall Farm (south of Goodwin's) 76 acres.
Hall Place Farm (next to the church) 132 acres.

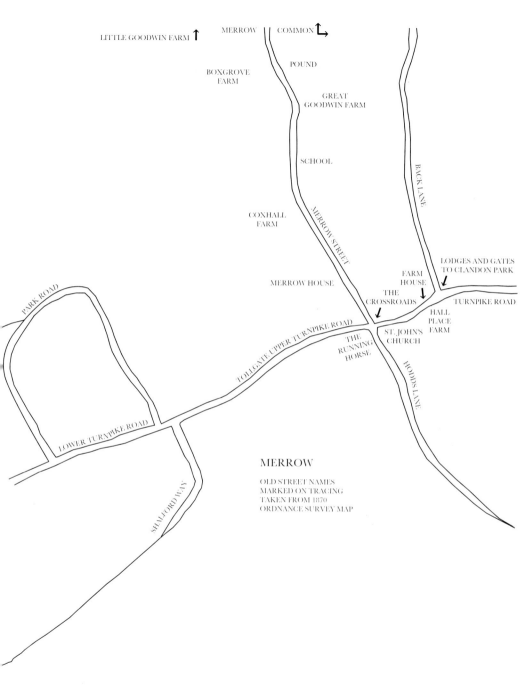

LITTLE GOODWIN FARM ↑

MERROW   COMMON ↳

POUND

BOXGROVE
FARM

GREAT
GOODWIN FARM

SCHOOL

BACK LANE

COXHALL
FARM

MERROW STREET

LODGES AND GATES
TO CLANDON PARK

MERROW HOUSE

FARM
HOUSE ↓

THE
CROSSROADS ↓

TURNPIKE ROAD

PARK ROAD

HALL
PLACE
FARM

TOLLGATE UPPER TURNPIKE ROAD

THE
RUNNING
HORSE

ST. JOHN'S
CHURCH

HODDS LANE

LOWER TURNPIKE ROAD

SHALFORD WAY

MERROW

OLD STREET NAMES
MARKED ON TRACING
TAKEN FROM 1870
ORDNANCE SURVEY MAP

Old street names marked on tracing taken from 1870 Ordnance Survey Map.

Merrow as shown on 6" : 1 mile Ordnance Survey Map of 1870.

From an engraving by Edward Smith

William Cobbett (from an engraving by Edward Smith in *The Place of Surrey in the History of England* by F.J.C Hearnshaw)

Map: the apportionments record the property as Hall Place Farm owned by the Trustees of Guildford Hospital and occupied by Thomas Swayne, whose family first leased the house from the hospital in 1766 and held the tenancy until about 1912. (Domestic Buildings Research Group (Surrey) 1993 Report No. 307)

MERROW THE OLD FARM HOUSE

E.M.BUTTS - NOV. '92

The Old Farm House, Merrow. Previously known as Hall Place Farm House. (Drawing taken from report by Domestic Buildings Research Group - Surrey)

"TOLL COTTAGE"

The original "Toll Cottage" marked the end of Lower Turnpike and the start of the Upper Turnpike Road when travelling towards the east "Marke" of Merrow. It consisted of two rooms only and an outbuilding. The first road steam engine came through the Tollgate preceded by a man carrying a red flag in 1863: it went through free of charge. The Toll was abolished in 1867 and the "Toll Cottage" was pulled down. The Harms family, who kept the "Gate" from 1861 to 1867, had a "Tare" board and the tolls were:-

4d a horse
10d per score of bullocks
5d per score of sheep
(Nightingale, 1990, p14)

Today's "Tollgate Cottage" is a rebuilt 19th Century cottage. It is of brick with tile-hanging on the front and sides and consists of two main rooms on the ground floor with an added kitchen at the back and three (formerly two) rooms above. (Domestic Buildings Research Group (Surrey) 1989 Report No. 3824)

Tollgate Cottage, 181 Epsom Road, Merrow, photographed in 1997. This building is on the site of the original "Toll Cottage".

In the 19th Century the buildings in Merrow Street included - on the west side -:

"The Cedars" : one of the early farmhouses.

"Merrow House" - built in 1802, a plain brick building with three stories. Merrow House was bought in 1853, with the adjoining land, by Joseph William Thrupp from Chilworth (who paid for the building of the original Merrow Street School). After his death his wife and daughter Adelaide continued to live in the house. Mrs. Thrupp died in 1886 and Adelaide lived there alone with servants until she died in 1908. (See Chapter Three & *Miss Thrupp Visited* by Anne Knee, 1984)

"Yew Tree Cottage" - a timbered 17th century cottage which was the huntsman's cottage who kept hounds for the Earl of Onslow.

- and on the east side of Merrow Street -

"Evergreen Cottage" (17th century)

"The Rectory", later known as "Stoodwell", (which was demolished in the early 1960s to make way for the development in Rectory Close).

"Merrow Street School" - which was built in 1853 and subsequently enlarged in 1880, 1886 and 1901.

"Great Goodwin Farm" - formerly associated with the family of Robert "Godyng" and known as "Goodyns".

"Coxhall Farm"- marked on the **1870** map. The Coxhall Estate in Merrow was to be sold by auction by Messrs. Nash & Son at the White Lion Hotel, Guildford on Wednesday, June 16th 1878.

The Boxgrove estate at Merrow, consisting of a farm-house and about one hundred and fifty acres of land, was situated in Merrow Street below and opposite Goodwin Farm. The name almost certainly derives from Boxgrove in Sussex where a Priory was founded in the 12th Century. The friars there also held land in other parts of the country including Merrow. They established a farm in Merrow Street, reputedly in the mid-13th Century, and it was shown on maps as Boxgrove Farm until 1823. It had passed into private hands when the farm buildings were demolished in about 1856. The name "Boxgrove" reappeared on the western side of Merrow. (Knee, 1993)

North of Great Goodwin Farm was the Pound in which stray animals were impounded. (Gould, 1951, p3/16) [In December 1997 the *Surrey Advertiser* reported that proposals for a four-bed-roomed house at Pound Cottage on the west side of Old Merrow Street had been turned down amid calls to protect the village pound!]

Houses along the Turnpike Road on the northern side, going west from **the crossroads**, included:-

"Mayor House" - an early timbered house, which stood on the site of the present parade of shops - Nos. 221-229 Epsom Road. Mayor House was a general stores and bakery in the Swayne and Kimber families for generations - it was demolished in 1963.

"The Walnuts" - still exists. It was once a guest house and tea rooms and now houses Lloyds Bank.

"Garden Cottage" - still exists. Next to "The Walnuts" and built in 1780. The late Mr. Jack Gould believed that the first school in Merrow started in "Garden Cottage" in 1800.

"Forge Cottage", and The Forge itself, stood on the site of the present petrol filling station. The Cottage was demolished in 1955 and the last remains of The Forge, the horseshoe-shaped brick arched entrance, in 1968. The original Forge Cottage, an early half-timbered house, was a blacksmith's house for more than a century.

"Halldeane" (or Hall Dene) - built in 1856 (demolished in 1973).

Merrow Street School photographed in 1997.

Great Goodwin Farm House, Old Merrow Street, photographed in 1997.

mass; 28 other bonfires could be counted as dots of fire: rockets and fire balloons were also sent up. (This fire was one of 2,594 throughout the country.) Village festivities also took place at Levelsgrove, as already described. (Gould, 1948, p8/9).

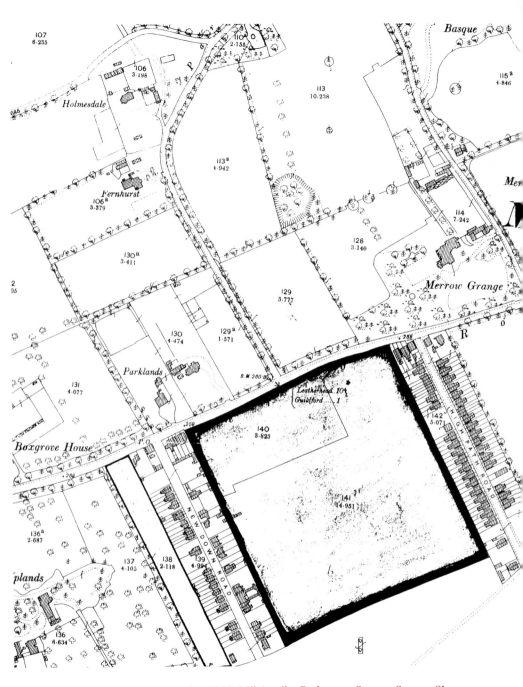

Merrow as shown on the 1896 25":1 mile Ordnance Survey Surrey Sheet XXIV.13.

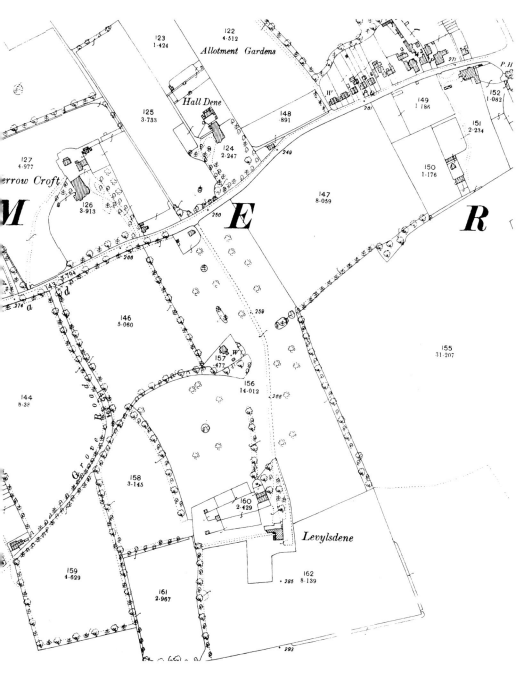

123
1·424

122
4·512

Allotment Gardens

271

P. H

Hall Dene

125
3·733

148
·891

W

149
1·186

152
1·082

127
4·977

124
2·247

249

151
2·234

errow Croft

M

126
3·913

250

E

147
8·059

150
1·176

R

266

143   3·794

d

146
5·060

259

R

155
31·207

274   a

157
·477

W

156
14·012

144
8·3?

Grove Road

266

158
3·145

160
2·429

Levylsdene

159
4·629

161
2·967

162
285   8·139

293

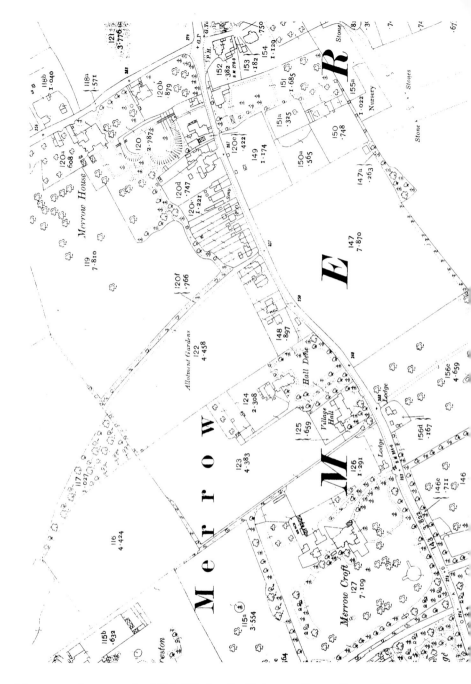

Merrow as shown on the 1915 25": 1 mile Ordnance Survey Surrey Sheet XXIV.13.

155b
2·873

Stone

155
26·990

Stone

181a
2·155

162
11·371

162a
·343

Levylsdene

156b
·410

156a
·136

31·207

160
2·757

156
4·912

157
458

161a
·418

146a
1·710

161
2·703

146b
·673

158
2·504

158a
·734

Fryfield

144a
2·450

159
1·507

159a
1·472

Thorn Chase

Golf Club House

144
5·949

159b
1·032

Mission Room

142b
2·110

142a
·769

159c
·633

G o l f   C o u r s e

CHAPTER TWO

THE FIRST HALF OF THE TWENTIETH CENTURY

Just as William Cobbett wrote about Merrow in the early 19th century, so Rudyard Kipling wrote about it in his *Just So Stories* in 1902 :-

> *There runs a road by Merrow Down -*
> *A grassy track today it is -*
> *An hour out of Guildford Town -*
> *Above the river Wey it is.*

[See Chapter Five]

It is believed that Rudyard Kipling was at Newlands Corner when he wrote those lines, staying with John St. Loe Strachey, Editor of *The Spectator*, in the house "Newlands Corner" which Mr. St. Loe Strachey (a future Sheriff of Surrey) had built for himself in 1892 looking out over the view that he thought the finest in Surrey. (Parker, 1952, p249). The Stracheys ran their house from April 1915 to March 1919 as a 24 bed Auxiliary Red Cross Hospital.

By 1901 Merrow had a population of 1,320 and this rose to 1,690 in 1931. Merrow became part of the Borough of Guildford in April 1933 (when Guildford town more than doubled its size to 7,180 acres). (Chamberlin, 1970, p26). Merrow village, therefore, took on the role of Guildford suburb but retained many features of independent village life. (See Appendix No. 3 for later population figures.)

The **1915** edition of the 25":1 mile Ordnance Survey map shows the main road from west to east as "Merrow Road" and it retained this name until 1930 when it was widened and renamed "Epsom Road". Merrow Road was tarred in 1909. To the south of Merrow Road there is little change since 1896: only a house called "Firfield" to the east of Grove Road and two large properties between the southern end of High Path Road and the Golf Course on Merrow Downs - the Golf Club House and "Thorn Chase".

Going in a westerly direction along the northern side of Merrow Road from **the crossroads**, there are 3 pairs of semi-detached houses and one other property on the field south of the allotment gardens next to "Hall Dene". On the western side of "Hall Dene" (formerly Halldeane) there is the village hall which was built in 1909 and cost £695.16s.0d. The house north of "Merrow Croft", formerly known as Basque" has been renamed "Freston".

Today's Horseshoe Lane was then still known as Park Road.

In the early 1900s several cottages were built in Merrow Street including Appletree, Coxhall, Garnet, Michaelmas, Peace, Orange and Gateside Cottages. Spring Cottages were built in 1912 and The Myrtles in the 1920s. Merrow Street was tarred in 1911.

The road between the church and the inn [formerly known as Hodds Lane) is known as "Trodds Lane" on the **1915** map. This was named after the Trodd family who lived there for many years.

The **1915** map shows 9 properties on the eastern side of Trodds Lane near the Downs: 2 pairs of semi-detached and one other property fronting on to Trodds Lane and 2 pairs of semi-detached properties behind them (fronting on to today's Swayne's Lane). It also shows the Cricket Ground and a Miniature Rifle Range to the east of the churchyard. On the western side of Trodds Lane there was no new development (6 houses shown on the **1896** and **1915** maps).

In 1914 Mr. John St. Loe Strachey of Newlands Corner offered a prize for a model cottage to be built at low cost for working class housing and agricultural labourers. The architect, William Clough-Ellis, won the prize and his wooden cottage still stands on Merrow Common. It cost about 100 guineas to build and is now known as No. 3 Model Cottages. Later 3 more cottages of similar design were built in brick on the site - only one of these remains - No. 2 Model Cottages - which has been restored and extended.

The **1934** edition of the 25":1mile Ordnance Survey map still refers to the main road as "Merrow Road" although the name was changed to "Epsom Road'" at about this time. Between St. John's Church and the Cricket Ground the farm buildings of Hall Place Farm are no longer shown. In their place are five detached houses, the most easterly one of which was to become The Rectory. On the eastern side of Trodds Lane south of the church much development has taken place. There are six houses in "Abbots Way" and five houses in "Three Pears Road", all with large gardens. 6 more properties have been built along the road to be named "Swayne's Lane". Between Swayne's Lane and the Downs there are 12 houses, the most southerly four in larger grounds than the other eight. A Tennis Ground is shown near the Cricket Ground but not the Rifle Range.

On the western side of Trodds Lane there are a further ten houses, including four off a new road called "Downsway" (subsequently increased to 12).

On the southern side of Merrow Road, between the crossroads and "Levylsdene" the **1934** map shows a small road (to be known as "The Paddock") and a new road called "Fairway" (shaped like an upturned Y)

Merrow as shown on the 1934 25": 1 mile Ordnance Survey Surrey Sheet XXIV.13.

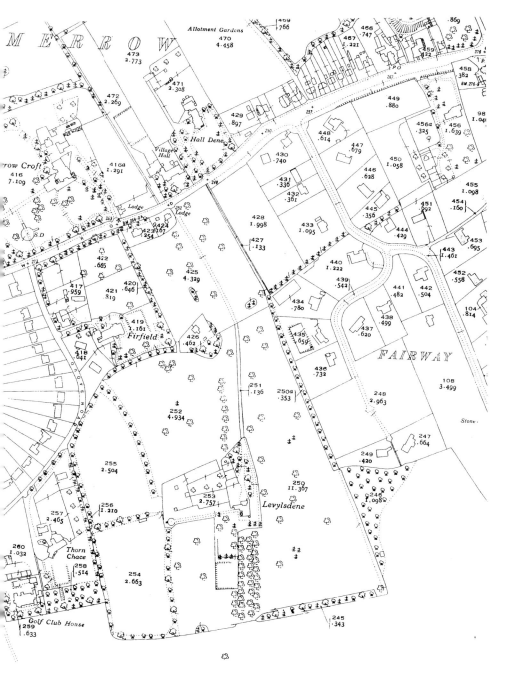

with over 20 houses with large gardens. Subsequently the houses in Fairway doubled in number. Between "The Paddock" and "Fairway" on the Epsom Road were the "Old Stables", which are believed to have been built in 1936 as stables for racehorses although they may never have got further than housing a few hacks. The stables had a thatched roof. (Subsequently converted into six bungalows in 1958.)

Continuing in a westerly direction, 3 more houses have been built near "Firfield" and there are 16 detached houses on the western side of Grove Road and 4 more houses before High Path Road fronting on to Merrow Road.

Further development has taken place between High Path Road and Down Road (no longer "New" Down Road). Holford Road, Elles Avenue, Carroll Avenue and Daryngton Drive are shown on the site of a former market garden. There are over sixty new houses shown on the **1934** map, mainly in Daryngton Drive and on the Downs side of Elles Avenue. All these roads have subsequently been fully developed.

To the north of Merrow Road: the **1934** map renames "Park Road'" as "Horseshoe Lane". A handful of houses are shown inside the "horseshoe" (to the north and west of "Merrow Grange"). "Merrow Grange" became an hotel in the early 1930s and was well known for its wedding receptions, dances and riding facilities. During the Second World War it became an auxiliary hospital (1941-45). To the north west of Horseshoe Lane between "Woodlands" and "Holmesdale" a new road called "Woodway" is shown with 6 houses in large gardens. South of "Fernhurst" a house called "Greencroft" has been built.

A further 19 houses are shown between Boxgrove House (at the junction with the main road) and Boxgrove School on the eastern side of Boxgrove Road [being the western boundary of Merrow]. Some of the houses front on to Boxgrove Road and others on to 2 new roads - Green Lane and Meads Road.

As mentioned in Chapter One, Boxgrove School in Boxgrove Road, which had opened in 1881 with just three pupils, had grown to about 40 boys by 1906. At this time the school was purchased by Mr. H.F.H. Caldwell, a Scottish business man. Over the next ten years he further enlarged the school with the erection of buildings for staff and boys' accommodation, a dining hall, laboratories, a workshop and a school chapel. This was situated right at the corner of Boxgrove Road and Boxgrove Lane. The school changed hands again in 1926 and the adjoining farm and land were purchased to increase the size of the school estate to 44 acres.

The school continued in being during the second world war with reduced numbers but after the war these rose to a maximum of 135 boys. In 1963 the whole estate was sold to builders and after a period all the school buildings were demolished and the development of Boxgrove Park commenced. (Knee, 1993) [See also Chapter Three].

Returning to **the crossroads** and the eastern side of Merrow Street, the **1934** map renames the house next to Merrow Street School (formerly known as "The Rectory") as "Stoodwell". Further north: on the eastern side of Park Lane at Merrow Common there are 7 more properties (including the Model Cottages mentioned earlier), and on the western side of Merrow Street "Carthouse Cottages" have been built.

By the 1930s there was a comprehensive bus service within the Borough of Guildford to and from the centre of the town including buses along the Epsom Road.

The house known as "'Uplands" on the southern side of the Epsom Road, and west of Down Road, was built in the 1860s. Until the 1950s, when changes were made to St. John's Church Parish boundary, "Uplands" was in the ecclesiastical parish. Now the site is outside but adjoins the western parish boundary at the allotments at the back of houses on the west side of Down Road. (See Chapter Three).

Colonel Lane Fox (who later became a Lieutenant General and changed his name, in 1880, to Pitt Rivers when he inherited the estates of his great uncle, George Pitt, 2nd Baron Rivers) lived at "Uplands" from 1873 to 1877. During this time he excavated a mid-2nd Century AD round Bronze Age barrow and six Saxon barrows on Merrow Downs (south of Levylsdene). (Merrow Residents' Association, 1991, p5).

It is rumoured that "Uplands" is haunted by the ghost of a young serving girl who fell from an upstairs window whilst being chased by an amorous suitor in the very early 1900s!

At the outbreak of the Second World War "Uplands" was empty and ripe for requisition by the Government under emergency powers. A number of huts were erected in the extensive grounds and the buildings were used by a number of Government Departments. After the war it became one of the London periphery dispersal sites to house government employees and the standard type of single storey brick offices were put up: they were built this way so that they could be turned into an emergency hospital should the need arise. Large chunks of the Ministry of Food were brought to "Uplands" from their war-time HQ at Colwyn Bay between 1948 and 1950 and the Epsom Road site was bought by the Ministry of Works in 1951.

(*The Uplander* No. 329, Jan. 1986. p2 - M/AF&F). The staff brought down from Colwyn Bay lived on site at first. The men were lodged in the wooden huts and the ladies were accommodated in the old house and other brick buildings. When the Bushy Hill estate in Merrow [see start of next chapter] was built many houses were ear-marked for the "Uplands" staff.

Known as "Government Buildings" the "Uplands" buildings are the administrative and divisional offices of the Ministry of Agriculture, Fisheries and Food. The administrative offices deal with the payments to farmers and horticulturalists and with the Ministry's statistical and accounting work. The divisional office gives advice to farmers and growers in Surrey and East and West Sussex. (Borough of Guildford Official Guide, 1982-84, p56).

The "Government Buildings" eventually filled the site. Most of the buildings are one-storey only but there is one taller block near the Downs which has **not** improved the vista from the western end of Merrow Downs!

"Uplands" House (1861) photographed in 1997. The house is now in the centre of "Government Buildings" in the Epsom Road.

"Uplands" House surrounded by "Government Buildings" is shown centre left in this aerial photograph taken in 1987. The Epsom Road is clearly shown in the centre of the photograph which looks towards Guildford. (Copyright: P.T. Sherwood)

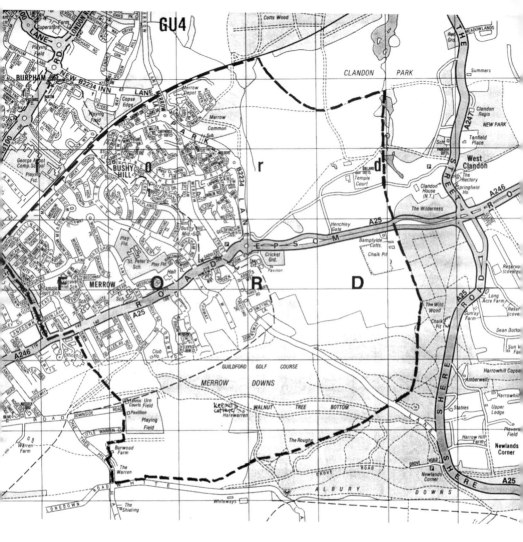

Part of Page 61 of the 1990 *Surrey Street Atlas* reproduced by permission of Geographers' A-Z Map Co Ltd and with the permission of The Controller of Her Majesty's Stationery Office, © Crown Copyright Licence No MC88129M0001.

■ ■ ■ indicates the parish boundary of St. John the Evangelist, Merrow, which has been added to the map

36

Further south, on the eastern side of Merrow Street, "Rectory Close" was built on the site of the old Rectory.

On 22nd November 1947 the *Surrey Advertiser and County Times* reported that Merrow House - the three-storey square brick building on the west side of Merrow Street - was to be purchased by Trustees of the Poyle Estate and leased to a new Housing Society - "Guildford Sunset Homes". It was adapted to house elderly persons of limited means and officially opened in 1949.

This was followed in 1959 by the building of 92 flats to the north of Merrow house and this new development was officially declared open in July 1960. The 8 house blocks are named Pond, Paddock, Stile, Mares Field, Meadow, Poyle, Browell and Orchard Houses. There is also a small building called Thrupp House next to Merrow House named after the Thrupp family who lived there from 1853 to 1908.

After nearly thirty years as an old people's home, Merrow House closed its doors in 1978. It remained empty for six years until in 1984 conservation work started to make a number of single and double flats for elderly people.

In 1989-90, the site of the former "Hall Dene", on the Epsom Road next to the village hall, was developed as "Halldeane" (Home for the Elderly).

Continuing on the northern side of the Epsom Road: the old house "Merrow Croft" has been demolished and 27 houses built in the grounds with a new road (1953) called "Merrow Croft" leading off Horseshoe Lane East. Other post-war developments in the Horseshoe Lane area include Woodlands Park, Grasmere Close, Beechway, Greencroft and houses in Horseshoe Lane itself and in Holmesdale Close. The Merrow Woods estate was built in the 1950s.

Development on the site of the former Boxgrove School (on the eastern side of Boxgrove Road between Boxgrove Lane and the railway line) began in 1956. The roads in the "Boxgrove Park" development have the names of naval commanders, such as Beatty, Nelson, Collingwood and Cunningham. This may have been prompted by the fact that the original "Woodlands" house had been built by an Admiral and the road leading to it had become known as Admirals Lane.

More development has taken place on the eastern side of Boxgrove Road, Meads Road, Green Lane and along the northern side of the Epsom Road 10 houses have been built west of Parklands. Parklands Place was built in the 1950s.

South of the Epsom Road there is another post-war development in the grounds of "Levylsdene", which were sold for building in 1955 (between Fairway and Grove Road). Like "Fairway", "Levylsdene" is shaped like an upturned Y with one of the prongs being named "Merrow Chase". These two roads have seventy privately owned houses off them and some flats.

Between Fairway and Levylsdene a road called "Tollgate" was built in 1959 (across the Epsom Road from Tollgate Cottage). On the Epsom Road on the other side of Fairway the former thatched stable block was converted into six bungalows with a green tiled roof in 1958.

"Longmead", off Grove Road, has 33 houses and houses have been built on the south side of the Epsom Road east of Daryngton Drive.

Off Trodds Lane on the west side there is Greatford Drive.

The next 6 paragraphs discuss schools and churches.

Bushy Hill School (for 7 - 11 year olds) in Sheeplands Avenue was built in 1955.

The foundation stones for the hall and Merrow Methodist Church, on the corner of Bushy Hill Drive and Sheeplands Avenue, were laid on 25th September 1954 and 30th March 1968.

In Horseshoe Lane East there is St. Peter's Catholic Comprehensive School (for 11-18 year olds) which was created in 1971 following the closure of St. Peter's Independent Boys School (situated on the site of the present school) and Merrow Grange Convent Girls School. The house around which St. Peter's School has developed was shown on the 1896 Ordnance Survey map as "Basque" (see Chapter One). From October 1945 until 1971 Merrow Grange was run as an independent girls school - "The Convent of the Ladies of Mary".

Part of the grounds of Merrow Grange were sold in 1983 for the building of a block of luxury flats with garages. St. Pius X Roman Catholic Church was built on the site of the Merrow Grange cowsheds, loose boxes and haystore in 1972 and later Laustan Close was built on former grazing land. The Merrow Grange building was eventually sold for residential development in 1993. All the school buildings were demolished with the exception of the original house. They were replaced with blocks of flats. The interior of the house has been divided into individual apartments, but the mock Tudor facade remains. (St. Peter's Catholic Comprehensive School Silver Jubilee brochure 1971-1996, p8/9).

St. Thomas of Canterbury Roman Catholic Primary School in Horseshoe Lane West was built in 1966.

Down Road School closed in 1967 and Boxgrove Primary School in Boxgrove Lane (for 5-11 year olds) opened in September 1967.

The Epsom Road shopping parade in Merrow extended to Bushy Hill Drive in 1968. There are other shops in the Epsom Road at the junctions with High Path and Down Roads and more shops in Merrow Park, Bushy Hill and Boxgrove Park. In 1969 the railway halt at Merrow was closed.

The **1994** Ordnance Survey Pathfinder Map No. 1206, at the end of this chapter, shows Merrow as it is today.

Across the Epsom Road from the lodge gates of Clandon Park is the Merrow Cricket Club (founded before 1857). Nearby is the Tennis Club and St. John's Rectory (232 Epsom Road).

The June 1997 issue of the parish magazine of St. John the Evangelist, Merrow *"Crossroads"* had a description of the parish boundary walk which took place on Rogation Sunday, 4th May 1997. Dorothy Seymour, whose description it was, has kindly agreed that I may quote from it:

"Our route took us across Clandon Park and Merrow Common to the railway which marks the parish boundary as far as Boxgrove Road. Skirting Merrow Park estate along Great Goodwin Drive and Merrow Woods, we ended up at 11 Boxgrove Lane ... It was bright and sunny as we continued along the parish boundary up Boxgrove Road to Merrow Downs, passing the allotments and noticing that most of the holders were growing rhubarb. Once over the open Downs it is impossible to follow the actual boundary, so we continued along One Tree Hill Road to Burwood Farm enjoying the extensive views towards Pewley Downs and the Cathedral. The pathway alongside White Lane led us up towards Newlands Corner where we should have found the Parish Boundary Marker (it was there three weeks ago) but somehow managed to miss it.

"Enjoying the quietness and beauty of the countryside we continued through the mainly wooded section of the Downs, along the hedgerow ablaze with yellow broom across Trodds Lane, the golf course (missing the golf balls) and open fields to the Wild Wood. From here we had glorious views towards Woking, Chobham and, in the far distance Heathrow Airport. It was here that we found the Merrow Parish Boundary/West Clandon Boundary Marker dated 1899.

"The final part of our walk took us through the Wild Wood with the beech trees in their fine spring greenery, past the quarry and alongside the cricket ground (a match was in progress) back to the church hall."

Merrow still seems to have plenty of allotments in the village not only the ones mentioned above near Down Road, but also a much larger area in the hub of the village, across the Epsom Road from the church on the north eastern corner of **the crossroads**. The aerial photograph clearly shows the extent of the allotments in the bottom right hand corner. They provide an unspoilt, peaceful (and productive!) area in the village centre.

This map of Merrow has been reproduced from the Ordnance Survey
Pathfinder 1206 Map (TQ 05/15), (© Crown Copyright 1994), with the
permission of The Controller of Her Majesty's Stationery Office, © Crown
Copyright Licence No. MC88129M0001.

CHAPTER FOUR

MERROW DOWNS

In 1991 the Merrow Residents' Association compiled a Chronological History of Merrow Downs. Their History gives the area of the Downs as 155.96 hectares (385 acres) [Surrey Act 1985]. The map at the end of the Chronological History outlines the area of Merrow Downs. They extend from the path leading to The Ridgeway and the gardens of the houses near-by over the Golf Course (and the old Race Course) over Trodds Lane and some way to the east of the Shere Road near the hotel north of Newlands Corner. The southern boundary of Merrow Downs is the same as that of the golf course for some of the way but goes south of the area known as "The Roughs". Their northern limit adjoins the gardens of houses at the top of roads on the south side of the Epsom Road and follows much of the Golf Course boundary.

The geology of the Downs in the simplest terms is described in the Residents' Association History as consisting of a layer of chalk some 500 feet thick inclined upwards to the south at an angle of 10 degrees. This layer ends abruptly at the south facing escarpment at Newlands Corner (567 feet).

There are several hundred yew trees on the Downs and four or five have girths of over 20 feet. One yew tree near Newlands Corner is recorded as being 2000 years old. This tree can be identified from the service tree growing from the centre of it.

Sir Richard Onslow bought Clandon Park from Sir Richard Weston in 1641 and at some later date the Onslows extended their estate and acquired Merrow Downs from the Westons. The Downs then remained in the ownership of the Onslow family until 1967 when they were purchased by Guildford Borough Council from the Earl of Onslow (subject to the lease of the land to the Golf Club).

The Hare Warren built by Lord Onslow in Walnut Tree Bottom on Merrow Downs in the 18th Century consisted of an area of several acres enclosed by a six-foot high flint wall. The wall can still be clearly seen surrounding and extending to the south of Keeper's Cottage in Walnut Tree Bottom. The hares were bred for hunting and food. Two or three of the artificial "meuses", which were about 5 inches square and built into the bottom of the wall can also be seen. "Meuses" are the openings or gaps in a

fence or hedge made by hares through which they habitually pass and
through which they run for "relief" when hunted. Keeper's Cottage is to
the south of and roughly in line with the 11th tee of the Golf Course and
the site is marked on the **1990** Street Atlas.

The area along Walnut Tree Bottom near the Hare Warren used to be
described as "Fairyland" and this name was used by local people until the
1930s.

From 1701 to 1870 Guildford Races, flat and jump racing, were held annually in Whitsun week on Merrow Downs. The first official race was held in
1727.

The two mile course ran along the north side of what is now the 10th fairway of the golf course, up past the north side of the 10th green and round
towards the 14th green. It crossed the 3rd fairway near its teeing ground
and ran eastward, parallel to the 3rd fairway and just to the south of it. The
footpath below the ridge follows the line to Trodds Lane. It swung north
east before crossing Trodds Lane, ran some 200 yards south east of the 7th
green to within 45 yards of the Clandon/Newlands Corner road, swung
north west round the ancient yew trees and back along what is now a diago-
nal path and right of way west-south-west across the 8th fairway, crossed
Trodds Lane, ran up the 10th fairway and, finally, swung round to the east
of the chalk pit and "through a part railed in to the stand to the termin-
ation". The grandstand is believed to have been on the south side of the
course at its western end a few yards east of the 12th green. (See **1870** map)

There is an oil-painting attributed to James Seymour (1701-1752) in the
Green Drawing Room at Clandon Park titled "Harriers on the Downs near
Guildford" which shows the stand and a small part of the course near the
finish. The Onslow family at Clandon Park supported the Races on
Merrow Downs and Richard Onslow, the third Baron, who succeeded to
the title in 1740, was the chief supporter and Steward of Guildford Races.

On 15th June 1764 *Gimcrack*, a grey, won at Guildford. He won 26 races out
of 36 in 9 years. The Gimcrack Stakes run at the August meeting at York
every year is named after him.

The greatest racehorse of the 18th century, *Eclipse* , raced in "His Majesty's
100 guineas for Horses, not more than 6 years old, carrying 12 stone, four
mile heats" at Guildford on 5th June 1770: which was one of the 18 races
he entered as a five and six year old. He was named *Eclipse* because on the
day of his birth, 1st April 1764, there was a total eclipse of the sun. He was
foaled at the Duke of Cumberland's stud at Cranbourne Chase, near
Windsor. (Guildford Museum)

From GUILDFORD, 1896

And so with all thy faults, Guildford, I love thee still,
    Nestled beneath thy sheltering hill,
Surrounded by park-like lands and foliage green.
Nature has to thee been prodigal of wealth:
Pure, breezy downs, with sloping vales between -
Haunt of the golfer: where he may be seen
Pursuing pleasure, whilst recruiting health.

1896
Anon

From JUST SO STORIES

[The first six verses of the poem about Merrow Down come before the chapter *How the Alphabet was Made* and the last five verses are at the end of that chapter.]

    There runs a road by Merrow Down -
        A grassy track today it is -
    An hour out of Guildford town,
        Above the river Wey it is.

    Here, when they heard the horse-bells ring,
        The ancient Britons dressed and rode
    To watch the dark Phoenicians bring
        Their goods along the Western Road.

    And here, or hereabouts, they met
        To hold their racial talks and such -
    To barter beads for Whitby jet,
        And tin for gay shell torques and such.

    But long and long before that time
        (When bison used to roam on it)
    Did Taffy and her Daddy climb
        That Down, and had their home on it.

Then beavers built in Broadstonebrook
    And made a swamp where Bramley stands;
And bears from Shere would come and look
    For Taffimai where Shamley stands.

The Wey, that Taffy called Wagai,
    Was more than six time bigger then;
And all the Tribe of Tegumai
    They cut a noble figure then!

Of all the Tribe of Tegumai
    Who cut that figure, none remain -
On Merrow Down the cuckoos cry -
    The silence and the sun remain.

But as the faithful years return
    And hearts unwounded sing again,
Comes Taffy dancing through the fern
    To lead the Surrey spring again.

Her brows are bound with bracken-fronds,
    And golden elf-locks fly above;
Her eyes are bright as diamonds
    And bluer than the sky above.

In mocassins and deer-skin cloak,
    Unfearing, free and fair she flits,
And lights her little damp-wood smoke
    To show her Daddy where she flits.

For far - oh, very far behind,
    So far she cannot call to him,
Comes Tegumai alone to find
    The daughter that was all to him.

1902
Rudyard Kipling

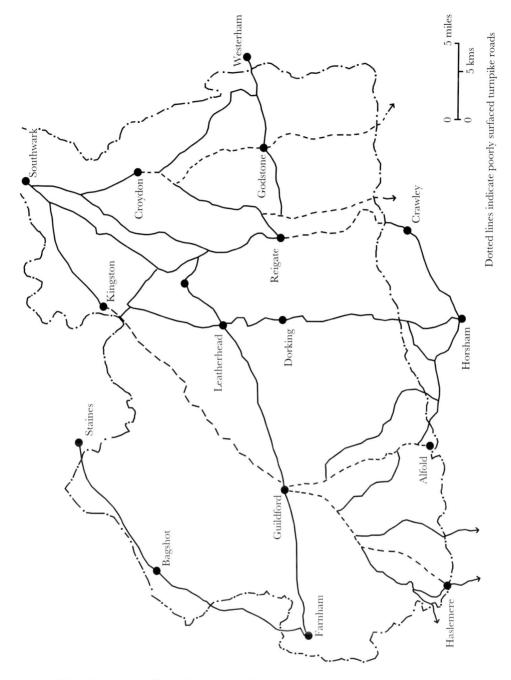

Map showing the Turnpike roads in Surrey taken from *A History of Surrey* by
Peter Brandon.

APPENDIX NO. 2

THE RUNNING HORSE

The following article appeared in Hone's " Every-Day Book," dated 1831 :—

THE RUNNING HORSE AT MERROW, SURREY.

The first point of peculiarity that strikes the traveller on approaching the " Running Horse " is the pictorial anomaly on the front of the house. The sign represents a racehorse with a rider on its back; but the painter has given us a horse *standing* as still as most horses would be glad to do after having been *running horses* for more than half a century. Our Running Horse, then, *stands* hard by the Church in the village of Merrow (*olim* Merewe), about two miles from Guildford, in Surrey, on the road leading from the latter place to London by way of Epsom. It is at the intersection of the high roads leading to Epsom, to Guildford, to Stoke, and to Albury, Shere and Dorking. The latter road passes over Merrow Downs, upon which, at the distance of a quarter of a mile from our hostel, is the course whereon Guildford races are annually held.

Guildford races formerly attracted a very numerous assemblage of spectators. The elderly inhabitants of the above-named ancient borough relate that, such was the influx of company, not a bed was to be had in Guildford unless secured some weeks before the sports commenced. From some cause, the nature of which the good people of Guildford have never been able · satisfactorily to ascertain, the races have gradually declined in celebrity and importance, and at present they are too often but thinly attended. The *programme* of the sports, which annually issues from the Guildford Press, is embellished with a woodcut, an impression, I believe, of the same block that has been used for the last century. The course is not considered by sportsmen a good one, but its situation and the views it commands are delightful.

When King George the First was at Lord Onslow's at Clandon, the adjoining parish, he gave a plate of one hundred guineas to be run for; and this is now the principal attraction to the proprietors of horses. The members for the borough of Guildford also give a plate of fifty pounds, and there is generally a subscription plate besides.

Our hostel, the " Running Horse " at Merrow, is the place of rendezvous for all the "running horses." Its stable doors bear highly characteristic and interesting trophies of the honours obtained by their former temporary inmates. The best-formed *pumps* that ever trod the floors of Almack's or the saloons of Carlton palace are not more delicately turned than the shoes (albeit they are of iron) which, having done their duty on the course, and brought their high-mettled wearers first to the winning-post, are now securely nailed against the honoured portals as memorials of his success. They are placed heel to heel, and within the oval is carved, in rude characters, the name of the horse, with the day on which he won for his master the purse of gold. What an association of ideas does the simple record convey. Here, on a fine warm evening in June, the evening preceding

> . . . " the great, th'important day,
> Big with the fate of jockey and of horse,"

arrived the majestic " Cydnus." His fine proportions were hid from vulgar gaze by cloths of purest white. As he walked slowly up the village street ridden by his jockey, a stripling of sixteen, his approach was hailed by the acclamations of the village boys and the calmer admiration of the men, all looking forward to their holiday on the succeeding day. " Here, I say; here, here— here comes one of the racers. There's a *purty* creatur, *law*— look at his long legs—*law*, Jem, I say, look what long steps he *do* take—fancy how must must *gallop*, if he walks *so—purty feller*. I'm sure he'll win—mind if he don't, now." Meanwhile the noble animal arrives at the inn door—high-breeding, whether in biped or quadruped, is not to be kept waiting. Out comes the host in an important bustle, with the bright key of the stable door swinging upon his finger. He shows the way to the best stall, and then takes his station at the door to keep out the inquisitive gazers, while the jockey and trainer commence their tender offices of cleaning and refreshing the horse after his unusual exercise of walking the public road. This done, he is fed, clothed, and left to his repose upon as soft a bed as clean straw can make, while the jockey and trainer adjourn to the house, the admiration of the knot of idlers who are there assembled to hear the pedigree, birth, parentage, education and merits of " the favourite." Other horses soon arrive, and the conversation takes a more scientific turn, while the jockies make their own bets, and descant learnedly upon those of their masters, till they betake themselves to rest, " perchance to dream " of the important event of the succeeding day.

Long before the dew has left the short herbage on the neighbouring Downs, the jockies are busily engaged in the stables; and before the sun's heat has exceeded that of an April noon they are mounted and gently cantering over the turf, with the double object of airing their horses and showing them the course over which, in a few hours, they are urged, at their utmost speed, in the presence of admiring thousands. What an elating thought for the youthful rider of the " favourite "; with what delight does he look forward to the hour. when the horse and his rider will be the objects of attraction to hundreds of fair ones' eyes glancing upon *him* with looks of admiration and interest, while, in his dapper silk jacket and cap of sky-blue and white, he rides slowly to the weighing-place surrounded by lords and gentlemen " of high degree." Within a short space the vision is realised— more than realised—for he has won the first heat " by a length." In the next heat he comes in second, but only " half a neck " behind. and his horse is still fresh. The bell rings again for saddling; and the good steed is snuffing the air and preparing for renewed exertions, while his rider " hails in his heart the triumph yet to come." The bell rings for starting. " They are off," cry a hundred voices at once. Blue and white soon takes the lead. " Three to one "—" five to one "—" seven to one "—are the odds in his favour, while at the first rise in the ground he gives ample proof to the admiring " cognoscenti " that he " *must* win." A few minutes more, and a general hum of anxious voices announces that the horses are again in sight. " Which is first?" " Oh, blue and white still." " I knew it; I was sure of it." Here comes the clerk of the course flogging out the intruders within the rails, and here comes the gallant bay—full two lengths before the only horse that, during the whole circuit of four miles, has been once within speaking distance of him. He keeps the lead and wins the race without once feeling the whip. Here is a moment of triumph for his rider; he is weighed again, and re-

ceives from his master's hand the well-earned reward of his
" excellent riding." The horse is carefully reclothed and led
back to the stable, where his feet are relieved from the shoes
which are destined to assist in recording, to successive generations
of jockies, the gallant *feats* performed by

> " Hearts that then beat high for praise,
> But feel the pulse no more."

Our hostel, however, must not be thus quitted. The date
inscribed within the circle above the centre window is 1615. The
house is plastered and washed with yellow; but its gables, Eliza-
bethan chimnies and projecting *bay* window (a very proper
kind of window for a " running horse ") render it a very
picturesque building.

PHILIPPOS.

November, 1827.

Article from Hone's *Every-Day Book*, dated 1831, about "The Running
Horse" at Merrow. This article was reprinted in *Merrow from Ancient Times* by
J. Gould (1951).

APPENDIX NO. 3

CENSUS RETURNS FOR MERROW FROM 1801 TO 1901

YEAR	POPULATION	YEAR	POPULATION
1801	169	1861	363
1811	181	1871	453
1821	240	1881	595
1831	249	1891	1,293
1841	252	1901	1,320
1851	278		

Merrow had a population of 169 in 1801, 1,320 in 1901, and 1,690 in 1931. By 1961 the population of St. John's Church Parish was 4,700. The figure rose to 6,300 in 1981 and to 8,650 in 1991.

The Merrow Residents' Association recently carried out a recount of the population in the ecclesiastical parish and the total figure for 1997 came out to 8,787 (in 3,579 residences).

APPENDIX NO. 4

RECTORS OF ST. JOHN THE EVANGELIST, MERROW SINCE 1800

RECTOR	INSTITUTION
S.Cole	1784
A. Onslow	1810
H.A. Bowles	1852
S.R. Flood	1884
H.V. Johnson	1900
A.H. Fletcher	1908
J. Palliser David	1923
F. Quirk	1929
L. Starey	1934
A.C.G. Oldham	1943
A.E. Ford	1950
A.G. Derbyshire	1967
R. Roe	1981
M.D.B. Lewis	1990
A. Hodgetts	1996

BIBLIOGRAPHY

Agriculture, Fisheries & Food, Ministry of, *The Uplander* No. 329 - January 1986.

Biographical Encyclopaedia of British Flat Racing , Mortimer, R.

Brandon, P. (1977) *A History of Surrey* Phillimore & Co. Ltd., Shopwyke Manor Barn, Chichester, West Sussex, PO20 6BG. [ISBN 0 85033 303 2]

Chamberlin, E.R. (1970) *Guildford - A Biography* , Macmillan and Co Ltd, London and Basingstoke. [Updated edition: Phillimore 1982]

Cobbett, W. (1830) *Rural Rides* [An abridgement with biographical introduction by E.R. Chamberlin (1982)], Constable & Co., London.
[ISBN 0 09 464060 2]

Cracknell, B. Sept./Oct. 1984 issue of *Surrey County Magazine*, published by Trevill, West Byfleet, Surrey.

Domestic Buildings Research Group (Surrey) Reports No. 307 and 3824 (with the owner's permission in each case).

Geographers' A-Z Map Co. Ltd. - see *Surrey Street Atlas*.

Gould, J. (1948) *Old Merrow with an account of the Church and its Bells* published privately.

Gould, J. (1951) *Merrow from Ancient Times* Woodbridge Press, Guildford.

Guildford, Borough of, Official Guide (1982-84), Home Publishing Co.

Guildford Golf Club - brochure.

Guildford Museum, Castle Arch, Guildford, GU1 3SX.

Hearnshaw, F.J.C. (1936) *Place of Surrey in the History of England* Macmillan and Co. Ltd., London, republished by S.R. Publishers Ltd 1971.

Hone's *Every-Day Book* dated 1831 - Article called "The Running Horse at Merrow" was reprinted in *Merrow from Ancient Times* by J. Gould in 1951.

Imms, Margery A (date unknown) untitled poem about Merrow Downs published in *Newlands Corner and its Environs* by D. Nightingale. [ISBN 0 9517094-1-0]

Janaway, J. (1994) *Surrey - A County History* , Countryside Books, Newbury. [ISBN 1 85306 309 6]

Kelly's *Directories of Guildford* (1959 and 1975) (Kelly's Directories Ltd. and IPC Business Press Ltd respectively).

Kipling, R. (1902), *Just So Stories* Centenary Edition, 1982, Macmillan London Ltd. (Literary Agents: A.P. Watt Ltd). [ISBN 0 333 32795 0]

Knee, A. (1983) *The Church of St. John the Evangelist, Merrow* and (1984) *Miss Thrupp Visited* - both published in Merrow.

Knee, P. and A. Notes on Merrow and some of its buildings deposited in the Muniment Room, Guildford and articles in St. Peter's Catholic Comprehensive School Silver Jubilee brochure.

Lewis, L. (1996) Poem entitled *Merrow Downs* published in *Poets in London and the Home Counties*, Arrival Press, Peterborough. [ISBN 1 85786 471 9]

Manning, O & Bray, W (1814) *The History and Antiquities of the County of Surrey*, Vol III.

Merrow Residents' Association (1991) *Merrow Downs - a Chronological History.*

National Trust *Guide to Clandon Park - The Family* by Pamela, Countess of Onslow (undated) Curwen Press, Plaistow, E.13.

Nightingale, D. (1990) *Merrow Village Then and Now* published by the late D. Nightingale.

Nightingale, D. (1994) *Newlands Corner and its Environs* published by the late D. Nightingale [Poem by Margery Imms].

Onslow, Pamela, Countess of - see "National Trust".

Ordnance Survey Maps :-
   6" : 1 mile, 1870
   25" : 1 mile, 1896; 1915; 1934
   Pathfinder 1206 (TQ 05/15) 1994

Parker, E. (1952) *Surrey Naturalist*, Robert Hale Ltd., London.

Phillipson, F. (1996) Notes deposited in the Surrey Local History Library relating to documents regarding Merrow Downs P.o.W. Camp in the Public Record Office, interview with former German P.o.W. and site visits.

St. Peter's Catholic Comprehensive School Silver Jubilee brochure (1996), Commercial Press Plc, Guildford.

Seymour, D. (1997) Article in *Crossroads* Parish Magazine of St. John the Evangelist, Merrow - June 1997.

Sherwood, P.T., ARPS Aerial Photographs.

Skinner, S. (1992) Poem called *Surrey Walk from Poet's England - 12 Surrey* Brentham Press, St. Albans. [ISBN 0 905772 36 9]

Surrey Archaelogical Society, Guildford Branch (1976) - Map entitled *Guildford circa 1840* - showing Merrow in 1839.

Surrey County Council Leisure & Tourism Unit leaflet (1991) *A Guide to Merrow, East Clandon and West Clandon*.

Surrey Street Atlas (1990) 3.3" : 1 mile - page 61. Geographers' A-Z Map Co. Ltd.

Tupper, Martin (1840) Extract from *Old St. Martha's*.

Victoria History of the Counties of England - Surrey, Vol.III, reprint 1967.

Wedlake Brayley, Vol II 1850, Walford Revision, *A Topographical History of Surrey*.

INDEX

70